Fact-o-graphics!

# HUMAN BODY FACTS

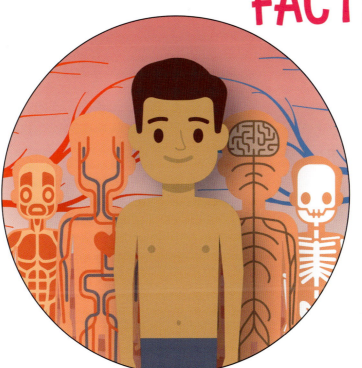

by
Emilie Dufresne

Minneapolis, Minnesota

*Library of Congress Cataloging-in-Publication Data*

Names: Dufresne, Emilie, author.
Title: Human body facts / by Emilie Dufresne.
Description: Fusion books. | Minneapolis, MN : Bearport Publishing Company, [2022] | Series: Fact-o-graphics! | Includes bibliographical references and index.
Identifiers: LCCN 2021005273 | ISBN 9781647479886 (library binding) | ISBN 9781647479930 (paperback) | ISBN 9781647479985 (ebook)
Subjects: LCSH: Human body—Juvenile literature. | Human anatomy—Juvenile literature. | Human physiology—Juvenile literature.
Classification: LCC QM27 .D84 2022 | DDC 612—dc23
LC record available at https://lccn.loc.gov/2021005273

© 2022 Booklife Publishing
This edition is published by arrangement with Booklife Publishing.

North American adaptations © 2022 Bearport Publishing Company. All rights reserved. No part of this publication may be reproduced in whole or in part, stored in any retrieval system, or transmitted in any form or by any means, electronic, mechanical, photocopying, recording, or otherwise, without written permission from the publisher.

For more information, write to Bearport Publishing, 5357 Penn Avenue South, Minneapolis, MN 55419. Printed in the United States of America.

**Photo credits:**
4 - MicroOne, 5 - Amaro_K, aliaksei kruhlenia, Anna Frajtova, Nina Buday, Prostock-studio, , 6 - Tridsanu Thopet, aliaksei kruhlenia, HappyPictures, Stocklifemax, 7 - Robert Kneschke, Iconic Bestiary, Vsevolod Shaposhnikov, Makc, 8 - Peter Hermes Furian, Nataliya Arzamasova, PosiNote, Egor Rodynchenko, eugenegurkov, Photoongraphy, 10 - Ger Bosma Photos, , 11 - Studio Barcelona, Laia Design Lab, Ser_bia, BlueRingMedia, Volha Shaukavets, gorillaimages, 12 - Sudowoodo, 13 - MicroOne, DarkestBlue, Glinskaja Olga, 14 - Panda Vector, Volkan Erdogan, 15 - Good Job, 16 - Andrey_Chuzhinov, elenabsl, 18 - Nataliya Dolotko, Rvector, 19 - AlZhi, Lucia Fox, Yurchanka Siarhei, 20 - Olesya Kuznetsova, Vasylyna Halun, Ivlianna, 21 - Alex Staroseltsev, Julia Tim, Sharlaev Maksim, 22 - Aksanaku, 23 - ankomando, Robert Kneschke.

Images are courtesy of Shutterstock.com. With thanks to Getty Images, Thinkstock Photo and iStockphoto.

# CONTENTS

The Human Body .................... 4
The Skeleton ..................... 6
The Senses ...................... 8
Muscles ........................ 12
Pumping Blood ................... 14
Breathing ...................... 16
Protecting Our Bodies ............ 18
Healthy Living .................. 20
Human Body Record Breakers ..... 22
Glossary ....................... 24
Index .......................... 24

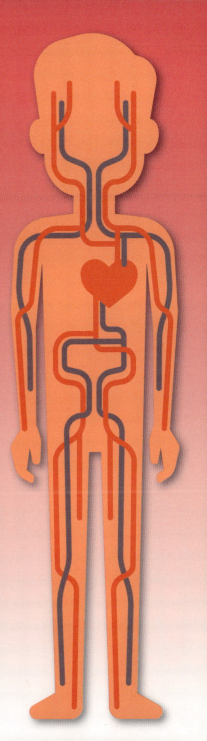

# THE HUMAN BODY

The human body is made up of lots of parts that all have different jobs. They work together to keep us healthy.

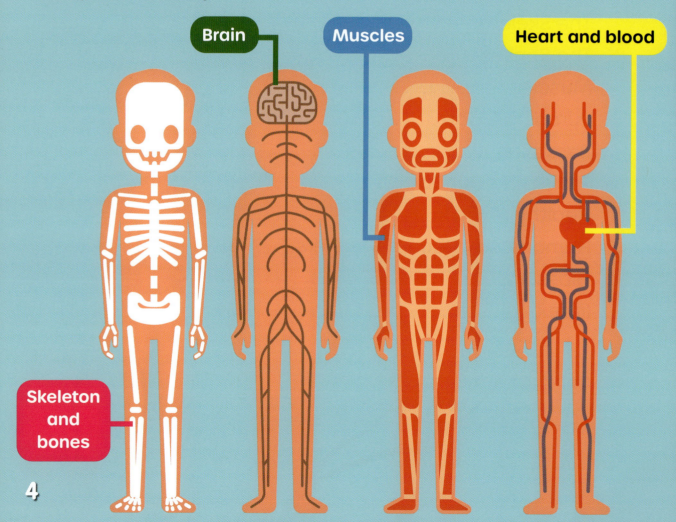

Our bodies need a few things to keep working. We need food to eat, water to drink, and air to breathe.

You can help your body by eating well and drinking water.

Exercising often, sleeping well, and finding **shelter** are also very important to a healthy life!

# THE SKELETON

The bones in our bodies make up our skeletons. Our skeletons hold us up. Without them, we would be like tents without poles—our skin and muscles would just fall to the ground!

A baby has about 300 bones. An adult has only 206! This is because some bones grow together as we get older.

To grow strong bones, we need calcium, vitamin D, and exercise.

Calcium is a **mineral** that helps bones grow. Milk has lots of calcium.

Our bodies make vitamin D from sunlight.

Exercise helps make bones strong.

Our bones grow until we are about 20 years old!

# THE SENSES

We have five senses. They are taste, touch, hearing, sight, and smell. Our senses work when different parts of our bodies send information to our brains.

## TASTE

Our tongue helps us taste. There are five main tastes: bitter, sour, salty, sweet, and **umami**.

# TOUCH

Our skin helps us feel the world around us. Here are some of the things we can feel when we touch things.

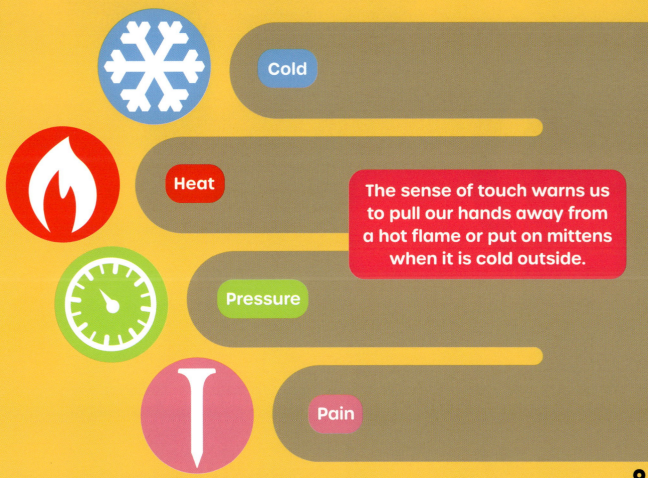

- Cold
- Heat
- Pressure
- Pain

The sense of touch warns us to pull our hands away from a hot flame or put on mittens when it is cold outside.

# HEARING

Our ears help us hear. This helps us know what is happening around us.

The inner ear turns the vibrations into messages that the brain can understand.

The outer ear takes in sounds and sends them to the middle ear.

The middle ear turns the sounds into **vibrations** and sends them to the inner ear.

# SIGHT

Our eyes help us see. In dark places, our pupils get bigger. This lets in more light. They get smaller to block out light when it is too bright.

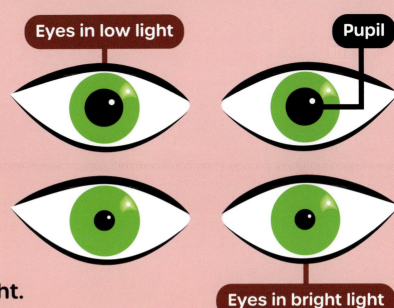

Eyes in low light

Pupil

Eyes in bright light

# SMELL

Our noses help us smell. They can help us know when something might be tasty or when it might be unsafe to eat.

# MUSCLES

Muscles help our bodies move. The human body has more than 600 muscles.

Muscles

Pairs of muscles often work together when we move. One will get tighter while the other gets looser.

Tight muscle

Loose muscle

The muscles attached to our bones give us the power we need to move.

Some muscles work without us having to think about them. One of these is our heart. We choose to make other muscles in our bodies move, such as those in our arms and legs.

Heart

Other muscles help us hold pee and poop!

# PUMPING BLOOD

The heart is just to the left of the middle of the chest. It is about the size of a fist.

Most people have more than 5 quarts (4.7 L) of blood in their body.

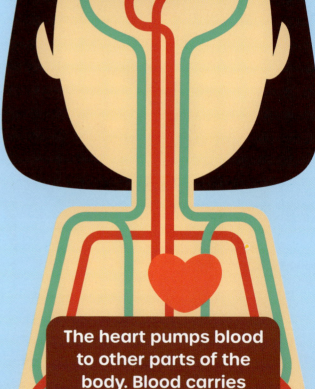

The heart pumps blood to other parts of the body. Blood carries **oxygen** and **nutrients**.

A person's heart pumps about 80 times every minute. It will beat about 2.5 billion times in a lifetime.

2.5 billion = 2,500,000,000

A woman's heart beats faster than a man's.

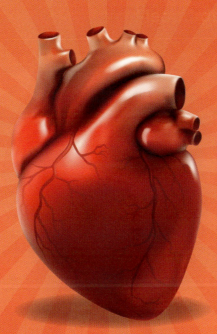

The heart can keep beating even if it is not connected to the body!

Every day, the heart pumps about 2,000 gallons (7,570 L) of blood.

# BREATHING

We breathe using our mouths, noses, and lungs. This is how we get oxygen into our bodies. Humans need oxygen to stay alive.

When we breathe in, air moves down the windpipe and into the lungs.

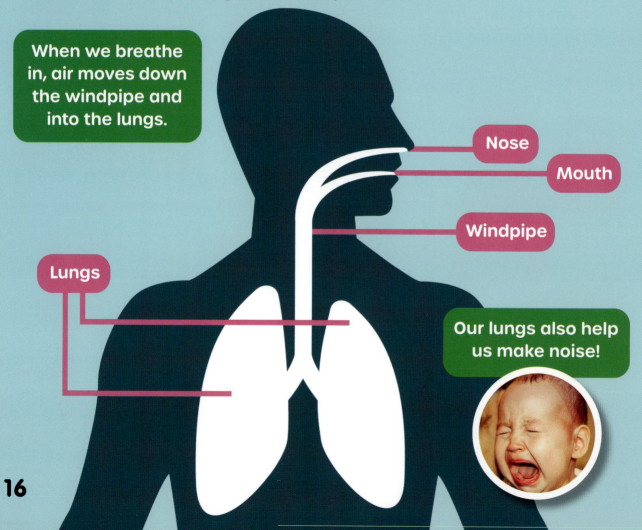

Nose

Mouth

Windpipe

Lungs

Our lungs also help us make noise!

# PROTECTING OUR BODIES

Our bodies are always trying to keep us from getting sick. Here are some of the ways our bodies help us stay healthy.

Our skin keeps bad germs from getting inside our bodies!

Before we are born, our mothers give us some of what we need to fight off sickness.

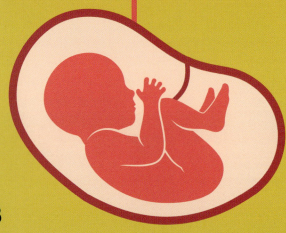

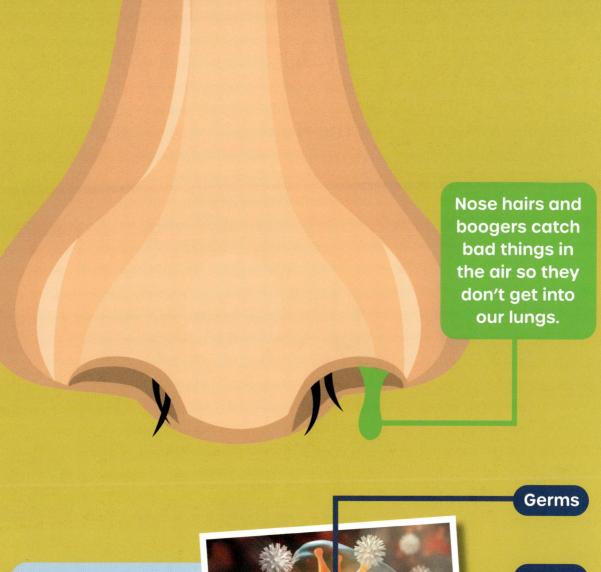

Nose hairs and boogers catch bad things in the air so they don't get into our lungs.

Sometimes germs get into our bodies. White blood **cells** fight them off!

Germs

White blood cells

# HEALTHY LIVING

It is important to eat the right foods in the right amounts. This keeps us healthy.

Beans, fish, eggs, and meat

Milk, cheese, and other dairy foods

Sugars and fats

Fruits and veggies

Potatoes, bread, rice, and pasta

20

Exercise keeps our bodies healthy. Try to exercise for 60 minutes a day.

Our bodies also need water to stay healthy. Try to drink water every day.

Exercise can also make us feel happier! It can help you sleep better, too.

# HUMAN BODY RECORD BREAKERS

Every person's body is different. Some human bodies break world records.

The largest feet ever were 18.5 inches (47 cm) long.

The world's longest human tongue is just over 4 in. (10 cm).

The longest head hair ever was more than 18 feet (5.5 m) long.

The world record for hula hooping without stopping is 74 hours and 54 minutes. That's a lot of exercise!

# GLOSSARY

**cells** the basic building blocks that make up all living things

**mineral** a thing that is important for good health and is found in certain foods

**nutrients** things that plants, animals, and people need to live and grow

**oxygen** something in the air that is needed for life

**shelter** a place to live

**umami** a rich taste found in many foods

**vibrations** fast, shaking movements

# INDEX

**blood** 4, 14–15, 19
**bones** 4, 6–7, 12
**eyes** 11
**hearts** 4, 13–15
**lungs** 16–17, 19
**pupils** 11
**taste** 8
**tongues** 8, 22
**touch** 8–9
**water** 5, 21

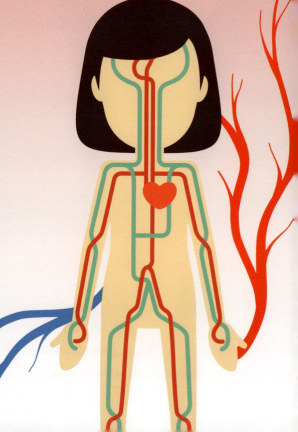